D1111825

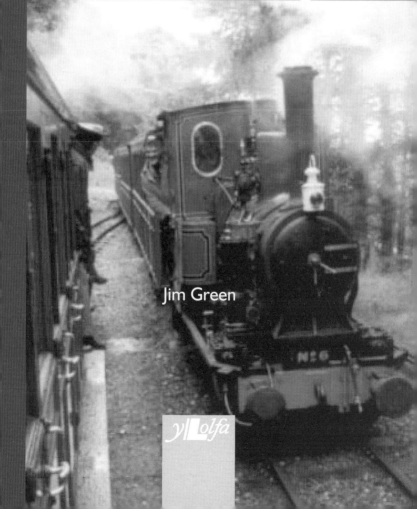

Welsh

It's Wales

Railways

Jim Green

y Lolfa

Photographs by the author.
Thanks also to Rod Phillips (p.51), Simon Fosbury (p.50),
Wales and West Trains and Ffestiniog Railway.

First impression: 2001
© Copyright Jim Green and Y Lolfa Cyf., 2001

Cover design: Ceri Jones

ISBN: 0 86243 551 x

Printed on acid free and partly recycled paper
and published and bound in Wales by:
Y Lolfa Cyf., Talybont, Ceredigion SY24 5AP
e-mail ylolfa@ylolfa.com
internet www.ylolfa.com
phone +44 (0)1970 832 304
fax 832 782
isdn 832 813

Contents

Introduction

Once upon a time… All the best stories I remember from my childhood used to begin with that phrase and when I heard it, I knew straight away that I was going to be told about somewhere wonderful, from a time when there were goodies and baddies and the goodies always won and, whatever happened in the story, there was always going to be a happy ending. If you are not old enough to remember train travel in the great days of steam engines and local branch lines and you were to ask about those days, then someone who remembers them might well tell you the story of those bygone days like this. Once upon a time everyone travelled by rail but trains were never crowded. Everything ran exactly to time and passengers were looked after by happy, cheerful, efficient staff who had all the timetables and platform numbers in their heads. Railway stations were places of charm, character and even magnificence. Travel was a joy and an adventure and when you got to where you were going you often felt sad that the journey was over. The great steam engines of the main lines were massive giants, every one, and were all bright paint and shining brass with billowing smoke and shushing steam. The branch-line trains, the slow trains as they were known, were pulled by little saddle-tank engines, 'puffers', that charmed children of all ages. They stopped at lonely halts and little local stations which were so carefully tended that they all seemed to have just won a prize for tidiness, or flower beds, or best of something. Carriages were bright and clean and the seats comfortable with framed pictures of all the exotic places you could visit by train hanging above them: Llandudno, Chirk Castle, Tenby. The railways were 'full of noises, sounds and sweet airs, that give delight and hurt not'. But this 'once upon a time land' never really existed like that, and what did exist was not to have a happy ending. What happened to the railways was not a Shakespeare comedy where everyone lived happily ever after: it was to be a tragedy. It was to finish a bit like a steam-hauled Hamlet where all the interesting characters get killed off. The steam locos went, lines closed, stations disappeared, a whole system seemed to shrink almost to nothing. Road traffic boomed and motorways got built and people deserted the poor old railway system for cars and buses. In Wales, where building railways had never been easy, many of the hard won lines were abandoned. Whatever their value to rural communities they were 'no longer economical'. Along with the decline of the railways came the end of large-scale quarrying. Quarrying slate was also 'no longer economical'. As the quarries closed so the little narrow-gauge railways that served them died. Everything pointed to a sad and permanent ending for steam-hauled trains in Wales. But, as it turned out, the decline of rail travel and the closure of the quarries wasn't the end. Enthusiasts emerged and banded together to save whatever could be saved. At first the preservation enthusiasts were, like train-spotters, regarded by the general public rather as figures of fun, certainly not people able to run any kind of railway line even as a hobby. Yet it was these groups of enthusiasts who began to re-write the ending. Not only that, they set out to re-write the story, they refused to let the steam-hauled railways die and disappear. The railways they saved and preserved prospered and became the 'once upon a time' railways everyone wanted to remember. The railways of Wales you will meet in this book – standard gauge, narrow gauge, preserved and main line – are a wonderland of cheerful staff, handsome engines and rolling stock and magnificent countryside. You will be shown journeys you can take where you will, indeed, be sad when they come to an end. This book itself is a throw-back to that happy age of steam. It is not an out-and-out journey which tries to tell you everything about Welsh Railways as they are today. It is more of an old-fashioned holiday excursion, a specially laid on trip – just for the fun of it.

Jim Green

April 2001

Welshpool and Llanfair Light Railway

When you see this delightful 2′6″ gauge railway you may think of it as just a little, local, preserved railway tucked away in the beautiful, rural countryside of mid-Wales. In one sense you would be quite right. For the many visitors who travel on it, the ride, the views, the engines and carriages are more than enough to make it a lovely day out. The motorists on their way to or from the seaside enjoy a break for refreshments in the tea rooms at Llanfair Caereinion station surrounded by the sights and sounds of a by-gone steam age. Photographers with complicated cameras compose clever shots at Welshpool station, under the hill, whilst children old and young snap the smoke-puffing engine arriving or leaving. But in another sense this railway is part of an international enterprise stretching from Russia and the Baltic, through Europe and Africa and the Caribbean down to Australia. This railway is now, and has been since its beginnings as a preserved railway, an international adventure.

The railway was opened in 1903 to serve the needs of the local farmers and country dwellers. As road transport improved, the railway, as a passenger line, declined and the passenger service was withdrawn in 1931. The line continued as a

Sunshine and steam up at Welshpool Station.

9

Tyrol and West African carriages ready to leave.

goods line but was finally declared redundant and closed in 1956. Almost immediately enthusiasts set about trying to preserve the line and in 1963, after a gap of 32 years, the restored line ran its first passenger service.

The narrow 2'6" gauge was never very popular in Britain and the equipment of those lines which used the narrow gauge, when they closed, often disappeared as scrap. To preserve the railway the early enthusiasts had to scour the world for 2'6" equipment. When all the engineering work was completed on the steep Golfa incline at the Welshpool end of the line it was necessary to import 6,500 suitable hardwood sleepers that had been located and acquired in Australia. Although two engines survived from the original railway there was no passenger rolling stock. A rather uncomfortable beginning for passengers was made with some 'toast rack' coaches obtained from the Admiralty. The name 'toast rack' came from the arrangement of the simple wooden seating which made the passengers look as if they were sitting like slices of bread in a toast rack! It was an improvement on the goods wagons, designed for coal haulage, in which the original enthusiasts had made their first runs, but not much.

A more suitable answer to the carriage question was eventually found in the Austrian Tyrol and the West African coast. The Zillertalbahn, a busy tourist railway in the Tyrol, donated some lovely, balconied, wooden-bodied coaches originally built in 1900-1. They were fully refurbished and taken into service and brought a piece of Tyrolean charm to the gentler, but still impressive, gradients of Mid-Wales. These carriages have a wonderfully authentic turn of the century Austrian look and are very popular with visitors, filling quickly on a mixed-carriage train. However, they have been subtly modified, the rear balconies have been slightly widened and the rear compartment doors made into wider double doors. Inside the carriage just behind a rear door a seat folds up. In this way and with the help of ramps at both terminus stations wheelchairs can be fully accommodated.

It has been known to rain occasionally in this part of Wales and for those rare days when more modern weatherproof carriages might be needed, the railway went to West Africa, to bring home carriages built in Gloucester in 1961 and sent out to Sierra Leone to celebrate that country's independence. They were saved from being scrapped when the African line closed. They are quite a rarity among narrow-gauge rolling stock being of fairly modern design.

Keeping the line open and equipped with everything it needs means that the world is constantly searched for equipment and stock. *Orion*, the biggest loco on the line, was built in Belgium for a Finnish railway and came to Mid-Wales in 1983. *Orion*'s size meant heavier trains could be hauled up the steep gradients of the line. *Sir Drefaldwyn*, an engine with a short wheel-base especially suited to the curves of the line, was built by Franco-Belge at Raismes in France, saw service with the German Military Field Railway during World War II, then went to Austria before turning up and acquiring a Welsh name in 1969. *Joan* came in 1971 from Antigua in the West Indies where she hauled sugar cane.

The buildings at Llanfair are as authentic as it is possible to make them allowing for the needs and comfort necessary for modern visitors. The original corrugated iron of most of the architecture was retained when the buildings were refurbished to a very high standard. It may never be possible for any building made of corrugated iron to be truly beautiful but the whole of Llanfair station, from the lovely tea room in the old Long Shed to the modern paved platform, has a charm that simply reeks of nostalgia and loving care.

The Raven Square station at Welshpool, on the other hand, looks quite different. Here the material of the buildings is the more traditional wood, equally well preserved and maintained. The main building was once Eardisley station on the Hereford, Hay and Brecon Railway. Built in 1863, it is typical of the standard design of hut for military and colonial use, then very common, now rather rare. When the Hereford line closed the building became a garden shed and then a pig sty before being rescued and rejuvenated and given a new lease of life fulfilling its original purpose.

Watching the world for equipment and learning how to repair, re-build and refurbish has given the staff at Welshpool a great pool of talent. And when the Soviet Union gave way to separate countries, the skills and knowledge gained in Mid-Wales found a new use. Frank Cooper, Deputy General Manager, through contacts made in buying stock, found that there was over 100,000 km of narrow-gauge railway in the old Soviet Union still in use but declining rapidly. Putting to use the skills and experience of buying stock and restoration work gained in his time at Welshpool, he began to help former Soviet Republics rediscover and put new life into their narrow-gauge lines.

And so the process goes on. The visitor only sees the lovely countryside, the beautiful Banwy river, the charming buildings and the marvellous old steam-hauled trains. And that is a great deal and certainly worth a day out. But behind it all lies a global activity, not only bringing narrow gauge into Mid-Wales from around the world but taking Mid-Wales' skills and expertise out to the world and sharing a truly remarkable adventure.

Fairbourne Light Railway

Fairbourne stands opposite Barmouth on the west coast of Wales. They almost touch each other but are separated by the river Mawddach. The Mawddach estuary is very beautiful and it is this beauty together with the long sandy seaside beaches which have combined to make Barmouth a popular and well established resort. Fairbourne shares the estuary and also has long, lovely beaches and, in its own way, is a resort. However, Fairbourne began life as a ferry station for both local people and for the pilgrims making their way up the coast to the great pilgrimage sites of Holywell, near Chester, and Bardsey Island which lies just off the Lleyn Peninsula in North Wales. The small island lying in the estuary is known as Ynys y Brawd, the Isle of Brothers, and was named after the monks who used to look after the ferry in medieval times. The monks disappeared at the Reformation and roads replaced the ferry as the main

Barmouth by ferry anyone?

form of travel between Fairbourne and Barmouth with a toll bridge providing a short cut across the river at Penmaenpool. But the ferry still operates today during the summer for visitors and crossing from Barmouth by ferry is, perhaps, the best way to visit Fairbourne and enjoy the railway.

The little Fairbourne railway owes it existence to the success of self-raising flour! Arthur McDougall, whose name is forever linked to that popular commodity, decided that Fairbourne could be developed as a resort. It had, after all, good access by rail for those living in the industrial West Midlands, long sandy beaches, wonderful scenery, mild winters and balmy summers. Rain didn't seem to be a problem for resort visitors in those days! McDougall was

On the way to Penrhyn Point.

not a man to waste money so he set up his own brickworks in Fairbourne and established a horse-drawn tramway to carry the building materials to where they were needed. It ran along the finger of sand which reaches out into the estuary and ends at Penrhyn Point.

Fairbourne flourished as a resort for a while and some industrial magnates built or bought villas there as summer residences for their families. In 1916 the line was taken over by Narrow Gauge Railways Ltd. and, with the help of the model-building firm Bassett-Lowke, the tramway was converted to steam and became an attraction for summer visitors. Time moved on and so did the visitors. Barmouth continued to flourish but Fairbourne settled down to a more humble role. But it still had visitors and the little line continued to run.

The 1939-45 war interrupted everyone's holidays and the histories about the line tell that, at the end of the war, the little line was badly damaged and unfit for use. Just why Penrhyn Point should have been a target for enemy action is not clear, but perhaps it was not the enemy who did the damage but lack of use and casual vandalism which made the line unusable. Whatever the cause the line was sold and began a new period of prosperity.

Post-war Britain was going to the seaside again and when it got there it wanted a bit of fun! The owners refurbished the line and invested in new locomotives and rolling stock and a period of prosperity and success followed. But times changed again and in the 60s the great British public discovered that there was sun as well as sand just a couple of hours flying away at the Costas in Spain. Fairbourne, like many other resorts, couldn't compete.

Enough visitors still come to Fairbourne to keep the little railway alive. Its appeal is that it is not so much a small real railway as a big toy railway. It doesn't attract the same interest and attention from enthusiasts as the preserved narrow-gauge railways and is excluded from the elite category of 'The Great Little Trains of Wales', but I'm sure it doesn't care. It is a fun railway where anyone who rides on it can become a happy, easily pleased, post-World War II child of the 1950s playing with trains. There is even something delightfully 50s about the tea shop café at Penrhyn Point and the dunes which surround the line.

Farbourne Station.

Riding on the little train out among the dunes, especially on a windy, overcast day, you might find yourself asking, 'Were children ever so easily and cheaply pleased? And were holidays ever really so simple as days in the dunes, wrapped up warm under grey skies by the seaside?' Of course they were. There's really not very much at Fairbourne, but if you are in the area a ride on the railway and a trip on the ferry shouldn't be missed. It's not exotic, you won't see it featured in the weekend colour supplements, but it's fun!

The Talyllyn Railway

Surprisingly, the Talyllyn Railway owes its existence to the American Civil War! Cotton producers in Manchester were suffering as a result of lack of cotton supplies from the southern or Confederate States of America. These had been disrupted by the northern or Union States' naval blockade which had been put in place at the outbreak of the war in 1861. The cotton producers badly needed new enterprises and the Aberdovey Slate Company was just such a new venture.

Building was booming as the industrial age gathered momentum and even the poorest workers living in the new industrial towns needed roofs over their heads. And it was Welsh slate that was the main element in providing the roofs over the heads of both the rich and poor in industrial Britain.

An Act of Parliament created the railway in 1865. Strangely enough, this was the year the American Civil War ended ensuring cotton supplies would be available again in the near future. The line itself was opened in 1866 and was originally designed to run down to Aberdovey to make use of

Drivers chat as trains cross on the Talyllyn line.

the harbour to transport the slate. However, the opening of the standard-gauge Cambrian Line made a junction of the two lines at Tywyn more economical.

The quarry and the line never really prospered but both survived until 1946. In that year the roof of the one remaining working quarry collapsed and the quarry closed down. The railway continued but closure seemed to be inevitable, especially when Sir Henry Haydn Jones, a local MP who had run both the quarries and the railway since 1911, died in 1950. The railway had, after the closure of the quarry, become a seasonal railway attracting visitors and enthusiasts. And it was the enthusiasts who met in Birmingham to form a preservation society.

Today preservation societies, formal and informal, exist to preserve just about everything from great houses and castles to varieties of domestic chickens, so it may be hard to realise just how big a project preserving an ailing old narrow-gauge steam railway was seen to be in 1950. Running a railway, even a little narrow-gauge railway, was strictly governed by laws going back to the beginning of the Railway Age. All railways had come into being by Acts of Parliament and railway legislation had continued at a fairly brisk pace for about 100 years.

Not only did people doubt enthusiasts' ability from an engineering and technical point of view, they doubted their ability from a safety point of view. Rail disasters were a part of the nation's popular memory. When things had gone wrong on the railways and people died, the headlines were always banner size. Nobody wanted people playing trains with other people's lives no matter how enthusiastic they were. But a society was formed and did preserve the railway.

At Talyllyn main station the justly proud boast is displayed, that the Talyllyn Railway is the oldest preserved railway in the world run by enthusiasts and volunteers. And you do get a feeling of enthusiasm when you ride on the Talyllyn Railway. The staff seem to really enjoy their work and their enthusiasm and enjoyment rubs off onto the passengers. Perhaps it comes from the fact that when the train finally gets to the end of the line it arrives at nowhere at all!

Just time for a snack before the train leaves.

Nant Gwernol is the terminus but there is nothing there, no shop, no toilets, no ticket office and no road access. There is no point in the train going there other than to come back! The reason for this is that the line used to finish one station down from Nant Gwernol at Abergynolwyn where the station has a café, shop and toilets. The train goes through Abergynolwyn and on to Nant Gwernol, then turns straight round and comes back one stop. The train takes a break of about half an hour at Abergynolwyn for the passengers to walk about and refresh themselves. The bit of line that runs up through the Nant Gwernol ravine is only there because the enthusiasts who run the railway wanted it to be as long as possible regardless of where it went! That, I suppose, is why they are called enthusiasts.

Another feature of the Talyllyn Railway is the variety of walks available alongside the line. A pleasant, reasonably short walk is that from the Nant Gwernol terminus back to Abergynolwyn station. This takes just about the same length of time as the rest stop the train takes and many passengers make the walk on fine days thereby giving some small purpose for the station at Nant Gwernol. Other walks from stations abound and the wooded countryside along the Afon Fathew valley is very lovely for walking or picnicking. Route guides for the walks are sold at the Tywyn station.

It has been known to rain during the summer in this part of Wales and some may think that wet weather is a disadvantage on a day out. This is not necessarily the case. Dolgoch station is very close to Dolgoch Falls. Falls of any description rely, for their effect, on the quantity of water going over them. A long dry hot summer may be beautiful for the beach but sunny, dry weather can render any waterfall a singular disappointment to visitors. "Is this it?" tends to be the response if the week previous to the visit has been hot and dry. However, a really good spell of wet weather can make the Falls behave in such a way that the visitor can see straight away why people take the trouble to come and look. The train travels over the gorge in which the Falls are situated just before it enters the station. Dolgoch Falls are only about five minutes from the station and no special footwear is needed for the walk. The gorge contains other falls worth seeing. However, to see these other falls some difficult walking is required and good walking footwear is necessary. If you decide to break your journey at Dolgoch station the Dolgoch Falls Hotel is not far away and serves refreshments and bar meals during the day.

Another feature of this railway is the chance to be a rich snob! For the payment of a £1 supplement each way it is possible to ride 1st class. The train is usually made up of three types of carriages. The 1st class carriage is fully enclosed with comfortable, upholstered seats with antimacassars over the headrests. Gentlemen don't wear macassar oil on their hair any more but it is a nice touch and makes you feel that bit more superior. The other two carriages are open-sided or enclosed. Both have adequate seating but not up to the standard of 1st class. The open-sided carriages undoubtedly give the very best views but, although roofed, are very much open to the weather. These carriages are the most sought after in warm sunny weather but only contain the hardy when it is cold or raining strongly.

The only opening windows in the enclosed carriages are the windows in

All ready driver?

the doors, which rise and fall using a leather strap with holes at intervals so the window can be set at different degrees of openness. If the window in the door nearest to you is open when you board the train, it is fun to try and fully close it using the leather strap. There is a 'knack' you need to know to close the window properly but I will leave you to work it out for yourself if you do not know it. It can pass the time whilst you are waiting for the train to start.

The Talyllyn line today is a lovely attraction for the visitor and an enduring monument to enthusiasm for railways. What began in 1951 is alive and well and in very good hands.

Vale of Rheidol Light Railway

Narrow-gauge railways were often built to carry things rather than people, coal or slate or building materials. They sometimes took on passenger traffic as a means of supplementing their industrial income. It was usually only after lines had closed and been re-opened as preserved lines that they became exclusively passenger lines serving tourists and enthusiasts. The Vale of Rheidol Light Railway is unusual in that it was always primarily a passenger line. It is true that The Manchester and Milford Railway obtained powers to build a railway from Aberystwyth to Devil's Bridge in 1861 to serve the various mines in the Rheidol Valley but no railway resulted from these powers.

First train of the day at Aberystwyth Station.

A railway was eventually opened in 1902 and some mineral wagons ran with passenger carriages but mining in the valley declined and, after the end of the 1914-18 war, the line became a purely passenger line. Indeed, the line can be said to have been a summer tourist attraction rather than a local service from very early in its history. From 1912 to 1922, with a break during the war, an engine had to be borrowed from the Ffestiniog Railway to deal with the summer traffic. In 1931 the winter service was withdrawn and the line became a summer only tourist line.

The steam engines cannot have been an attraction. Steam-hauled trains may be interesting and unusual today but up until the arrival of diesel locos they pulled trains all across the country. No, what people came to see then and still come to see is the enchanting Rheidol Valley. But today, when steam is the exception rather than the rule, the beautifully turned out engines and the quaint carriages are a particularly attractive bonus. The first train of the day begins from the Aberystwyth terminus which stands alongside the main railway station.

If you arrive about half an hour before the first train is due out you might be in time to see the train being assembled. The carriages are pulled out from their sheds by a diesel shunting-engine and then the beautifully turned out engine which will pull the train comes out and is coupled up. You can stand quite close by and watch all of this.

If you look at the front of the engine you will probably be surprised at how wide the engine seems for the narrowness of the rails. The gauge is 1 ft. 11¾ inches but the engine width is 8ft. and the weight about 25 tons!

The Rheidol Valley station and line sit alongside the main line terminus of the Cambrian Line. This is because, up until 1988, both lines were owned and operated by British Rail. The Rheidol line had been operated since 1923 by Great Western Railways who had become part of British Rail when the rail network was nationalised.

The popular tourist line was the last steam-hauled operation to be owned and operated by British Rail and it was very successful. However, the line was put up for sale in 1987 just as the passenger figures for the season were announced, up by 38% on the previous year and the best for seven years! If the financial logic of this decision escapes you, you are probably not alone.

If the weather is warm the best views are from the open carriages but the line climbs 680 ft in its 11¾ mile journey so if there is any chill to the wind wrap up warmly if you want the best view. I decided to sit in the open carriage which was the first one behind the engine. When the train pulled away I

Half way and taking on water.

suddenly felt a light spray on my face: it only lasted for a brief moment. It vaguely reminded me of riding on a log-flume at an amusement park many years ago but the spray was so light and fine it was in no way unpleasant. I couldn't work out where the spray had come from. I assumed it came from the engine, but where? When the driver blew the steam whistle again I saw that it produced a light spray which drifted past the carriage on the breeze, so that mystery was solved.

The Rheidol line runs alongside the main line up to the outskirts of Aberystwyth and then past outlying industrial units on one side and the river on the other. After crossing the main road at a level crossing and going over a river bridge the train pulls out into flat, quiet farming country. The river valley scenery is pretty but not exceptional although there is some interesting looking wetland on the river side of the line. Suddenly the river veers off to the left and the train moves into more wooded countryside and the climb begins.

There are no station stops on the Rheidol line but there is a stop to take on water after about half an hour. After that stop the train resumes its climb. Eventually, from high up on the valley side, you will be able to look down to where the river has been dammed and a reservoir created. A small way further on, by the river, are the remains of one of the old mineral mines. Now that the train is high up the views are wonderful as the train runs round the sharp bends where the line follows the curves of the mountainside. The train suddenly comes out of the forest to give clear views up, down and across the valley.

It was as the train went round one particularly sharp curve with the mountainside falling away sharply to the river far below, that I began to dwell on the very narrow gauge of the track and all that 25tons, 8ft. wide engine hanging out either side of the wheels. It's all perfectly safe but it added, for me, just a little thrill that went so well with the spectacular views. The line runs through deep rock cuttings as it nears the Devil's Bridge terminus and as you pass through the last narrow cutting you find yourself looking up at neat, separate little bungalows as the train pulls in at the Devil's Bridge station.

Devil's Bridge.

The train stops at Devil's Bridge for about an hour and you can walk and refresh yourself. Everything you need is at the station, café, toilets and shop. There is not much to do at Devil's Bridge but what there is can be done in an hour. The main attraction is the Falls which are about 200 yds down the road to the left of the station.

If the Falls do not interest you then you can turn right out of the station and walk along the main road. Not far along is a shop which is also a café. Beside the shop is a tea-garden which is a lovely place to sit and eat and drink if the weather is warm and sunny. After the break at Devil's Bridge the train begins the run back down to Aberystwyth, a beautiful run in truly beautiful country.

Bala Lake Railway

The Bala Lake Railway is a joy to look at and to ride on. It runs along the shoreline of Bala Lake, the largest naturally occurring lake in Wales, and it would be hard to find a better setting for a narrow-gauge tourist line. So it comes as no surprise to find charming little steam engines pulling the small open and closed carriages. And because a purpose-built tourist line seems so natural in this beautiful spot it may come as a surprise to find that the Bala Lake Railway did not begin life as a tourist line.

It was established in 1868 and eventually became part of the main line from Ruabon to Barmouth which was run by Great Western from 1877 until nationalisation in 1948. In 1965 the line was closed, the future being seen by the government of the day to be with road transport and motorways. Many rural lines disappeared at this time. But the line didn't stay closed for long and it was soon reborn to become a first in two ways.

George Barnes was a local engineer who, with the support of Merioneth County Council, registered the Rheilffordd Llyn Tegid Cyf./Bala Lake Railway Ltd. in 1971. This was the first company to be registered in the Welsh language. When the line was re-laid it also became the first narrow gauge

What's in a name?

All bright and shiny.

railway to be re-built over standard-gauge track line. Others would soon follow, but Bala was first.

The passenger rolling stock was all designed and built for the new little railway but the two main steam locos had begun life as working engines at the beginning of the 20th century. They were both built for service at Dinorwic where there was a slate quarry which continued working up until 1967. One engine, *Holy War*, had been refurbished after the closure of the quarry and was eventually bought and brought to Bala by Rev. Alan Cliff, then Minister of Wrexham Methodist Church. After an overhaul it began its new role as a passenger service loco. What is it about steam railways that so ensnares the hearts of British clergymen? So often one finds one or more Revs. tucked away somewhere in the workings of a preserved railway. Are you nearer to God on the footplate of a steam loco? Some people obviously think so.

The other little steam engine, *Maid Marian*, finished her working life at Dinorwic in 1964, was bought by a group of enthusiasts and then worked at Bressingham Gardens in Norfolk and on the Llanberis Lake Railway before coming to Bala in 1975. The two engines, apart from their paintwork, look very much alike to the non-expert, although *Maid Marian* is anything but original having had various changes made and bits from other similar locos added, over the years. Whatever the purity of their pedigree both are very beautiful.

How could two such lovely engines be designed and built for coarse quarry work? Looking at them today, all bright paint and polished brass, it seems as if their only role in life could ever have been bringing joy to visitors. It is engines like these that make the Rev. Awdry stories about Thomas the Tank engine almost believable as fact rather than fiction. If any steam engines could really have talked to each other and to the drivers, firemen and rail staff it would have been *Maid Marian* and *Holy War*. Why *Holy War* has such an ill-fitting name is something of a mystery. I don't think I have ever seen a more inappropriately named engine. It is about the least aggressive piece of engineering I have ever come across. Perhaps it is more evidence of the eccentricity of most of those involved with steam power.

Ever since its opening the little railway has been a popular attraction. Its main station is at the far end of the lake from the busy streets of Bala. It is on the edge of the quiet village of Llanuwchllyn with a good car park and the usual conveniences. Many visitors feel that the best way to use the railway is to get off at Llangower station and go for a walk, enjoying the lakeside country at first hand. If you do this it is easy to pick up a later train at the same station and then finish your trip. There is ample opportunity for picnicking on the walks and at both stations. However, if walking isn't for you how about dreaming? The round trip lasts about an hour and, with views through the wooded banks across the lake to the mountains beyond, it is easy to gaze out and drift off into happy daydreams.

However you plan your journey on this charming little railway, be grateful to George Barnes and all the others from the past and present who saved such a delightful stretch of railway and keep it running for the pleasure of others in such a wonderful place.

Just the thing for a warm sunny day.

Llangollen Railway

There is a natural valley from Ruabon, on the main Shrewsbury to Chester line, which runs through the mountains all the way to Bala lake. The river Dee runs along this valley and the countryside all around is very attractive. Indeed the whole area has a long-established reputation for attracting visitors. However, the railway line which ran along this valley from Ruabon to Bala and then on along another valley down to Dolgellau and on to Barmouth was not just for visitors but for goods and passengers and was a working line from 1877 until its closure in 1965.

Today, Llangollen is a popular tourist centre. It is an attractive little town with much to recommend a visit both to the town itself and nearby attractions. The town was named from the church, dedicated to St. Collen, 'llan' meaning an enclosure around a place of worship founded by a monk. Just quite how active and successful these missionary monks of the 6th-9th century were is testified to by the very great number of place names in Wales which begin Llan... Llangollen had been a busy centre before the railway came. Above the railway station stands the canal wharf still in use today. The canal was built by

Llangollen's spectacular station.

that tireless civil engineer Thomas Telford to carry the industrial commerce of the area. The railway, when it was built, soon replaced the canal in this task as railways did all over Britain. But the Llangollen canal survived and shares with the railway the same valley down to the main line.

Not far away, at Chirk, canal and railway pass side by side high over the river Ceiriog by aqueduct and viaduct. Not far from the canal and the railway station at Chirk is the castle, still forbiddingly fortress-like externally but, continually inhabited, splendidly domesticated inside and surrounded by pleasant gardens. The Llangollen canal, like the railway, is for pleasure only now and there are cruises available from the wharf above the station including some which are horse-drawn. Other places of interest for the motorist arriving at or leaving Llangollen are the Horseshoe Pass and the beautiful medieval abbey remains of Valle Crucis to the north. Dinas Bran castle, to the east, stands high above the A5 and is accessible to those who like a tough uphill walk.

Not far from Llangollen is the ancestral home of the Yale Lordship from where the father of Elihu Yale set out to become a Pilgrim Father in America. Elihu Yale helped found the university which bears his name but returned to die in Britain and his tomb is now at the main parish church of Wrexham.

Llangollen is as popular as a visitor centre today as it has been since Victorian times. Mr and Mrs Gladstone chose to visit the area when touring by barouche and stayed at the village of Llandegla, north of Llangollen, at the Crown Inn.

A ride on the Llangollen Railway would be a lovely centrepiece to any visit to this wonderful area. The train runs on a standard-gauge line and everything, including the livery of the engine and carriages, is a reminder of steam-hauled British Rail in the days before the car became the supreme form of transport and dealt the death blow to rural rail lines in the 60s. The station is quite different from those of the narrow-gauge lines. It is longer, bigger and doesn't have the feel of a preserved line although that is exactly what it is. It is also situated in an excellent spot, right beside the river, near the main road bridge and opposite an old corn water-mill now converted to a restaurant and bar.

Arriving at Carrog.

After heavy rain the river Dee can look very spectacular as it surges along between the station and the mill and on under the bridge. For anyone who ever travelled by rail in the 50s this will be a wonderful time-trip backwards and for anyone too young to have travelled in those distant times this will be a fascinating and fairly accurate insight into what rural rail travel was like up to just after the middle of the last century. The brass and paintwork of the engines shine much more than they ever did in the hard working heyday of steam rail but the carriages have an air of cared-for but much-used shabbiness that is entirely authentic. First class carriages have a corridor and a toilet but many other carriages are separate from each other and without any connecting corridor. Those often-spoken wise words of advice from untold numbers of parents to their children when they were travelling come surging back, 'Be sure and go to the toilet before the train starts, you can't get out of the carriage once we're moving'. Still very good advice today!

The train pulls slowly out of the long station and past unused rolling stock. It runs alongside a section of the river often used for white-water canoe competitions. Eventually the train crosses a bridge and the river moves from the left side of the train to the right and stays on that side for the whole of the journey. From the train you will see, dotted about the countryside, handsome villas set among the trees. This part of Wales has, for a long time, attracted the well off who want a quiet, well-situated, country retreat after a life of successful hard work. You will also see the isolated farm buildings from where the fields of grazing sheep and cattle are worked. And you may, at some point, see a buzzard out for a day's hunting.

After about 10 minutes the train makes its first stop at Berwyn. The river is crossed here by a footbridge known as the Chain Bridge, for reasons which will be obvious, and which leads to the Chain Bridge Hotel. Not far from here are the Horseshoe Falls, a spillway which diverts the waters of the Dee so that they can feed the Llangollen canal at its beginning. The train goes on and suddenly pulls away from the river and goes into quite a long tunnel. If there are no lights it becomes utterly black and the old saying about not being able to see your hand in front of your face becomes quite true for a few minutes. Once out of the tunnel the train pulls on through the lovely wooded, hilly

Was it really just like this? Of course it was.

countryside, never leaving the river valley. It travels through the small halt of Deeside where it doesn't stop.

It is all so easy to gaze out of the window and look at the houses and farms and think of this train serving these remote communities before road travel became the norm. It may be quite hard however for the modern mind to accept that once the pace of travel could be as slow as the gentle chugging of the train. There is no sense of hurry and urgency becomes impossible. It is wonderfully relaxing. Whether it relaxed or frustrated those passengers for whom it was the only way to and from Llangollen for business or shopping all those years ago is now a matter for speculation. Railways like this were once such a common feature of the landscape across Britain and are now so rare.

Whatever one feels about the dominance of the road today it is wonderful to be able to slip back to a more leisurely pace for a time and feel oneself in another age when sixty miles an hour, a mile a minute, was regarded by many as dangerously fast and travelling was often just as important as getting there. The Llangollen line was never part of a famous mainline with fast trains pulled by record-breaking engines like the famous *Mallard*. This is that other well known piece of steam-rail history, the 'slow train'. It still stops at empty stations like Glyndyfrdwy where, even on a busy day, hardly anybody can be seen. Yet the station is clean, tidy and well-presented, not in the least derelict or uncared for. The whole line has that sense of enthusiasm and pride which was so characteristic of rural steam railway when it was at its best and seems so lacking anywhere in railways today.

Finally the train rolls into its terminus at Carrog station which has been beautifully re-built to fit the period of the line. The Llangollen line is preserved but still very much alive. There is a special train called the *Berwyn Belle* on which you can dine, either luncheon or dinner. You can ride on trains that provide music and dancing. You can have a go at driving the engine or use the whole train as a corporate day out. A joint canal/rail trip can be organised and overnight stops with rail travel days included. You can play the stock market and buy shares in the company.

The Llangollen Railway may be a nostalgia trip for some, a piece of history for others, or just an excellent day out, but it is very much alive and well and providing a wonderful addition to all the other many attractions clustered in and around the town of Llangollen. The great British public may have discovered other exotic, far away places to visit since air travel became widely available, but this part of Wales remains as popular as it was in the days of Mr Gladstone, and rightly so thanks in no small part to the lovely 'slow train' of the Llangollen Railway.

Heart of Wales Line

There shouldn't still be a main railway link running directly between Swansea and Shrewsbury. It should never have survived the cuts and rationalisations of the rail network. But, thank heavens, the Heart of Wales line is still open and operating. If you begin your journey with the first weekday train from the Shrewsbury end you will see the train come in and unload a healthy number of passengers. They have come into town to go to work or go shopping or to use the other amenities available in the town. However, summer visitors and local people hardly seem sufficient for this lovely line to be kept going. Very much the same could be said about the Swansea end of the line. The nearer the train gets to Llanelli and Swansea the more passengers get on to travel to these important centres. Both ends of the line might produce enough local passengers to justify local trains but when you travel on this beautiful line it is hard to see how the line as a whole survives.

Certainly if the beauty of the countryside which a train passes through was enough to keep a line going then the Heart of Wales line would be one of the safest in Britain. When the train pulls out of Shrewsbury it quickly runs into the gentle, rural Shropshire countryside and, before long, reaches the area known as the Shropshire Alps which lie behind Church Stretton. These lovely hills and the long high shoulder of land known as the Long Mynd rise up steeply from the surrounding farming country and are a very popular place for visitors. Much of the line between Craven Arms and Llandeilo is wonderful walking country and in the days of British Rail extra Sunday trains were provided in the summer for the many walkers who used the line to reach walks otherwise difficult to get at.

When the train leaves Church Stretton it continues on the main line to Craven Arms where the Heart of Wales line turns west towards Wales. From here on the line is single track. This is quiet country and not far away just over the hills to the right of the train are the villages of Clunton, Clungunford, Clunbury and Clun, 'the quietest places under the sun' according to the 'Shropshire Lad' poet A. E. Houseman. The train runs on through the sleepy

Running over Knucklas viaduct.

little villages of Broome, Hopton Heath and Bucknell, all with request-stop stations, pretty cottages and snug-looking pubs. If you hear a buzzer sound twice it means the train driver has spotted a passenger waiting at a request stop and is alerting the guard. In darkness the driver will blow the whistle as the train approaches so passengers can come out and be seen. It's all very friendly on this line.

Just beyond Bucknell the train leaves England and enters Wales and arrives at Knighton. Knighton is a lovely town, lost among the hills and woods of the border. It stands on the line of that ancient fortification Offa's Dyke and on the banks of the river Teme which will wander on its way into England and pass under Ludlow castle before joining the Severn below Worcester. Knighton cannot really be said to be near anywhere nor on the way to anywhere but it is well worth a visit if only to see the countryside which surrounds it.

Once across the border the land becomes less rolling and more hilly and not long after leaving Knighton you cross over from one side of the valley to the other by the spectacular viaduct at Knucklas. The train now runs higher on the valley side and on overcast and rainy days the clouds will hide the wooded hill-tops to remind you of just how high you are but you will be given lovely views down the valleys. Once past Knucklas the landscape becomes empty of human presence although the views are wonderful. You realise what a very lonely job farming in this kind of countryside must be.

It would be lovely to travel on this line in winter when the snow is on the ground and the leafless trees afford clearer views but the line closes from January to March so only unseasonal weather would provide such a treat. You may very well see a buzzard or a fox going about its business and, if you are lucky, you may even see a red kite gliding across the sky. Travelling on through the sparsely populated landscape the train suddenly comes to the beautifully kept station of Dolau. Here, on a small plaque on a fence by the platform, the origins of the line are remembered, 10th October 1865, 125 years of rail, it must have been put up in 1990.

The train runs on going over bridges which cross and re-cross one of the many little rivers that come down from these mountains to run into the river Ithon and on into the Wye. There are no road bridges on this part of the line because there are no roads hereabouts to cross. Eventually the line runs down into the spa-town of Llandrindod Wells where Friday is market day and the train is always that bit busier with enthusiastic shoppers.

Llandrindod Wells, together with Builth Wells just further on down the line, were Victorian spa-towns. In the hey-day of spa cures they were popular resorts and the railway must have been very busy. Both are still attractive places which work hard to make sure their visitors are made welcome and have plenty to do and see. Llandrindod Wells station looks very much like a Victorian spa-town railway station should look. This is not surprising, however, as it was re-Victorianised in 1990 using grants from British Rail Community Trust, Radnor District Council, Powys County Council and the Development Board for Rural Wales. Llandrindod Wells is very much a self-consciously Victorian town and in the month of August for a whole week the townspeople put on appropriate costumes and the town re-lives its Victorian past. For passengers ready for something to eat or drink it will be pleasant to note that the buffet trolley comes on board at Llandrindod Wells.

The next station is Builth Road for Builth Wells and it is interesting to see that the old station buildings, dating from 1865, are now all private dwellings. Once out of these spa-towns you are back into open country and rivers and you begin the climb up towards Sugar Loaf tunnel. But just before the train goes through the tunnel it stops at Llanwrtyd Wells.

Llanwrtyd Wells once had a famous sulphur spring which attracted visitors but it is now the smallest town in Britain with around 700 inhabitants. Although it may be small, very small in fact, Llanwrtyd Wells has an importance that goes beyond the borders of Wales, beyond Britain in fact. It is the venue for both an International Four-Day Walk and the World Bog-Snorkelling Championships! Not content with that fame it also hosts the Mid Wales Beer Festival and is home to the Red Kite Visitor Centre. It seems that the residents of Llanwrtyd Wells have given themselves entirely over to pleasure, and who shall blame them? However, returning to the railway, it is at Llanwrtyd that the two trains working on the line meet, cross and change crews.

After leaving the station you soon pass through the Sugar Loaf tunnel and come out into wooded countryside. Not far on you pass over a valley on the Cynghordy Viaduct. Just before you come into Llandovery a lonely church overlooking the railway from the right announces the town and the train soon pulls into the rather unlovely station. On leaving you pass by the impressive

Following the river down to Swansea.

Llandovery Rugby Football Club ground. The team's name, the Drovers, is taken from the ancient importance of the town as a place where drovers congregated when making their way with their livestock to English markets.

Just when you think that the hills will go on for ever the train begins to run through a flat and wide river valley and passing through Llanwrda more houses begin to appear in the surrounding country. At Llandeilo the town stands above the station on a hill and cannot be seen from the train. However, on leaving, if you look back, you will see part of the town peeping out from its hill and the old stone bridge that leads out of the town coming steeply down across the river into the Tywi valley.

Cynghordy viaduct.

From now on, in amongst the woods, fields and rivers there will be signs that you are no longer far from an urban and industrial landscape. At Llandybïe there is a derelict overgrown industrial site.

As you travel on, the urban and agricultural landscapes begin to mix in a broad valley and you find yourself alongside a river again; this time it is the river Loughor, and there are frequent wetland sites alongside the track. After Pontarddulais the skyline lowers and the hills are soon gone. Another railway line begins to run alongside and a bridge carrying the heavy traffic of the M4 goes overhead across the lines. You see wide sweeps of reeds and marshes and the river becomes a tidal estuary. At the edge of the receding tide wading birds feed and in the water herons stand up to their knees waiting patiently for their next meal. The train finally pulls into industrial Llanelli and the transfer from the remote, quiet hills is complete. After a short stop the train reverses out of Llanelli and back around the estuary and inland until suddenly you find yourself entering Swansea and approaching the station where the train terminates.

Swansea has had its financial ups and downs. It has seen great prosperity and financial depression. But it has resilience and today, although the docks may not ring with busy shipping, they are very much alive. Like so many other docklands they are being given a new life as a visitor attraction. There is the Industrial and Maritime Museum alongside the marina and the Dylan Thomas Centre on the river banks. Swansea has plenty to offer the visitor at the end of one of the loveliest train rides in Britain.

Start at Swansea and visit Shrewsbury or start at Shrewsbury and visit Swansea. Do it whichever way round suits you best, but be sure that you make time to do it; you won't regret it.

Welsh Highland Railway

If you were asked to guess when the last public service steam-hauled narrow gauge railway was built in Britain, what sort of date would you give as an answer? Late 1800s perhaps, or some time between 1920 and 1930? How about 1997 to 2005!

The Welsh Highland Railway was opened to carry the public from Caernarfon to Dinas in 1997 with a programme to extend the line as far as Porthmadog by 2005. The original line began life in 1922, staggered along for fifteen years, gave a steamy gurgle, and died. It had never been strong. The Welsh Highland (Light Railway) Company was formed by a sort of merger between two railway companies who had operated on parts of what was to become the Welsh Highland Railway line and both were bankrupt, not a very auspicious start.

The line was meant to be part of the railway complex which operated in this north-west corner of Wales, a mixture of narrow-gauge, standard-gauge, quarry, commercial and passenger lines. It was to connect Porthmadog with Caernarfon. Enthusiastic but exaggerated passenger projections, continual shortage of cash, economic recession and war together with a wonderful inability to get the trains to run properly, if at all, meant that it never really got going and didn't last very long. But in its failure as a commercial operation were the seeds of its eventual re-birth.

If it had been fairly successful it might have lasted longer and died more slowly and disappeared completely like many other little rural railways. Because it was always in trouble, one way or another, its short existence was never straightforward. It had a sort of co-existence with other lines and companies especially the Ffestiniog Railway. Towards the end, in 1934, the whole line was rented out to the Ffestiniog Railway for the fee of £1 for the first six months and 'let's see what happens after that'.

The Ffestiniog Railway had just experienced something of a revival in passenger traffic and hoped that this might be repeated with the Welsh Highland Railway. Alas it never happened. The Ffestiniog company tried hard

Weekday diesel on the Welsh Highland Railway.

but everything seemed to go against them. Passengers didn't use the line, a nine-week strike at a quarry reduced goods traffic and after a few disastrous seasons the line's fate was sealed. The outbreak of the Second World war saw the now unused equipment of the line requisitioned and taken away and much of the line torn up for war use. But the Welsh Highland Railway wasn't finished yet, a problem it had always been and a problem it was still.

Although there was now no railway to run, the Ffestiniog Company found they still held the rental of it. They found themselves in the unusual position of being responsible for running a railway that didn't actually exist! In 1942 they were at last able to obtain release from their responsibility for the line and finally, in 1944, the whole Welsh Highland Railway company went into receivership. By 1950 interest in saving and restoring railway lines was beginning to grow. By 1961 a society attached to the line had been set up and, in 1964, the Welsh Highland Light Railway Ltd. was established. But where other lines were saved and developed nothing much happened to the Welsh Highland line. It looked as if the old jinx on the line was alive and well.

All that changed towards the end of the century. The Ffestiniog Railway was now a successful, restored tourist line. It too had suffered from the decline of the region after the war and been closed down but had been restored, reopened and prospered. It saw the possibilities for re-building the Welsh Highland Railway not just as a tourist attraction, although it could certainly fulfil that role, but as an appropriate part of the transport network in what was now the Snowdonia National Park. The line could not only be profitable, it could provide environmentally friendly transport for the communities between Caernarfon and Porthmadog.

If you think this is good you should see the Pullman!

Needless to say no-one had rushed to take over the business of the defunct old railway and it was still in the hands of the receiver. So in 1995 the Ffestiniog company once more took on responsibility for the assets and liabilities of the Welsh Highland Railway. Most of the trackway and bridges were still available to be re-developed. Backed by the Millennium Commission and with the help of enthusiastic volunteers trains began to run again out of the station situated near the slate-quay car park under the great walls of Caernarfon castle and run along restored track to the station at Dinas about 2½ miles away. This had been the end of standard-gauge line on the old railway from Bangor to Caernarfon and the place where the narrow-gauge began.

The carriages used on these trains are the usual open-sided type with wooden seats, used on many restored lines, and standard second class carriages. A special feature is the first class Pullman carriage for which passengers pay a

Arrival at Waunfawr.

supplement well-worth the extra if you want to travel in antique luxury.

On leaving Caernarfon a cycle track begins to run alongside the railway and keeps the train company until it is well-out of the town. The train runs out into open farmland with views across the Menai Straits. For the first years of the life of this railway visitors could come back again and again and see a new and different railway on each visit, growing and developing. First a short run to Dinas, then going on to the village of Waunfawr then on and on until the whole line, twenty five miles long, ran all the way under Snowdon and down on to Porthmadog. Temporary buildings would come and go, new track and buildings be opened, new sights, new stations, new rolling stock. For anyone interested in seeing a narrow-gauge steam/diesel-hauled railway re-emerging this would have been a truly thrilling time. A chance to see something being built which had seemed to have died for ever.

The phrase 'living history' has had overmuch use in relation to sites and situations but I think it is fair to say that if anything has a right to claim to be a piece of living history it is the Welsh Highland Railway which in the 21st century seems to have finally found the place it sought back in 1922 and, at last, laid to rest the failure which so dogged its first life.

Llanberis

Imagine someone standing in a place of great natural beauty, beside a long, deep blue lake surrounded by high mountains, woodlands and a wide, cloud-swept sky. It is remote, quiet and peaceful and the whole area is full of wildlife. Imagine that person looking around at all that glory and saying, "What we need to do here is to get rid of that forest so we can strip out all of the slate in those mountainsides. We can bring it down to the lake and put it on a train on a railway line which we could build and send it all to a purpose-built port at the Menai Straits. We'll make a great deal of money." No thought for the lost beauty, no thought for the environmental damage, no thought for the natural wildlife – money is all that counts, making a lot of money.

That is what happened at Lake Padarn and the smaller lake next to it, Lake Peris. The result was the massive Dinorwic slate quarry and other quarries which gouged out the valuable black stone from the hillsides overlooking the lakes. Of course it didn't happen just like that; no-one stood by the lake and then suddenly set about quarrying and building a railway from Llanberis to Port Dinorwic, as the port at the end of the line came to be known.

Lake Padarn

Getting up steam just below the inclined plane.

In fact, no-one is absolutely sure when slate mining began on the lakes' side, but as the industrial revolution got going building materials were needed in vast quantities. Supplying that demand became big business and many places which had great natural beauty soon became eyesores because they had something that industry wanted more than beauty. Coal mines, quarries and factories and crowded, dirty towns changed the face of the country.

It wasn't that Victorian landowners and businessmen didn't value beauty, natural or otherwise: they did. Those who could afford it made sure that they and their families had big houses in places of great natural beauty far away from the mess and squalor which their money-making ventures created. And ordinary people wanted and needed industrial work. Rural life in the early 1800s was cruelly hard and poverty was the norm. Pretty pictures of shepherds and milkmaids were decoration for the houses of the well-off. No-one would have paid to have the true rural realities on their living-room walls.

At its height Dinorwic employed over 30,000 men and the railway carried untold tons of slate out to the port on the Menai Straits. During full production in the quarries Llanberis must have been a very bustling but unlovely sight alongside the beautiful Snowdon mountains. But today, with the quarries closed and nature returned, Llanberis has again become a place of beauty and interest. The delightful little lake railway ran along its present route for the first time in 1972. The old line had been closed in 1961 and its track torn up and,

An old quarry, now a diver's delight.

with the locos, sold for scrap. A little lake railway was seen to be a worthwhile visitor attraction. Just across the lake Snowdon had its own railway up the mountain. But that run was always rather expensive and a smaller, much cheaper ride so close to the big attraction would surely be popular.

And so it was and still is; the two railways are both very busy during the visitor season. And industry is still very much a part of this area, but it is now the leisure industry. In addition to the Snowdon Mountain Railway and the Llanberis Lake Railway there are trips on the lake by steamer in the summer. The old, rather impressive quarry buildings are now a fine Welsh Slate Museum and there are craft shops. Many come for the water sports and there is a diving centre at the lake. The views of the whole area, whether from high up on Snowdon or down at water level alongside the lake bring home to the visitor just what a lovely part of the world this is.

The countryside around the lake is now the Padarn Country Park with walks, views and a variety of plant and animal wildlife. Much of the old quarry around the little railway station is now very interesting and even attractive. Just a few yards away from the station is a high-arched entrance through which you come into a spectacular space with soaring quarry walls above deep, still water. There is a rusting cable way above the water from which hangs an old slate tub among the trees which have grown at the water's edge. A stunning place now used by divers for recreation and training. The station sits below the old workings and, above the train as it pulls out, is the old inclined plane which used to bring the slate down the hillside to the train.

All in all Llanberis, today, is a delightful place with shops and attractions, two wonderful railways, a lake and beautiful countryside and views all around. Just imagine someone standing next to the decaying, dirty, derelict quarry and saying, "What we need to do here is tidy everything up, make it all very attractive and interesting, reinstate as much of the natural beauty as we can and build a lovely little lake railway so people can ride along the lakeside, pulled by steam engines, and appreciate what a truly lovely place we have made for them here." That's just what they did.

The Gwili Railway

The modern, re-established Gwili railway takes its name from the lovely river valley through which the present line runs. It is part of an original line which ran from Carmarthen to Aberystwyth. The company which began the line was the Carmarthen and Cardigan Railway company, the C & C. Back in 1857, when the first sod was ceremonially cut by Captain Lloyd of Dolhaiddin, it was decided to use the 'broad-gauge' of 7ft ¼inch of the Great Western Railway rather than the 4ft 8½inch standard-gauge. This was because the 'broad-gauge' was also the gauge of the South Wales Railway which was to connect at Carmarthen. When Great Western bought out the South Wales Railway in 1862 they converted it to the now universal standard-gauge. This forced the C & C to convert their line as well.

The C & C had never been strong, financially, and this new cost must have come as a severe blow to them and in 1881 GWR bought out the C & C.

It is often believed that the building of railways in the Victorian age was a bit like finding money – get an Act of Parliament passed to give you the right to build a railway, build it and sit back and watch the money roll in. That was true of some railway companies but by no means all of them. Smaller lines in difficult country, serving sparse communities and shaky mineral industries, often suffered and finally failed, or were swallowed

I'm the goods...

...and I'm the people.

up by the companies who owned and operated the profitable lines.

The Carmarthen-Aberystwyth line, when fully operational, must have been one of the most beautifully situated lines in Wales. After running up the Gwili Valley from Carmarthen it went on up the Teifi Valley, through Lampeter and on up to Strata Florida, where the monks of the medieval Cistercian abbey were said to have kept the Holy Grail, the cup used by Jesus at the Last Supper. From Strata Florida the line turned west and headed on down to Aberystwyth on the coast.

The line was still in use in the 1950s, after nationalisation into British Rail, taking families on holiday from the South Wales valleys northwards to the great Butlins Holiday Camp at Pwllheli. By the late 60s the line was only used for hauling milk from the Pont Llanio creamery and in 1973 the line was finally closed, another beautiful Welsh line gone, it seemed, for ever. However, in 1975 the Gwili Railway Company was formed to re-open part of the line and run it as a tourist attraction. They managed to obtain a Light Railway Order in 1977 and purchased an eight-mile section of trackbed. In 1978 the first passenger train of the new line ran with just one engine and one coach.

The story of the Gwili Railway from then on is one of more track, more stock and more passengers. People began to realise that dead lines needn't stay dead and that plenty of passengers still wanted to ride along the lovely lines if they could be re-opened. So the Gwili Railway grows and grows; just how far they will get and how long it will take remains something for the future. But, for today, a run along the lovely Gwili valley is enough and well-worth the visit.

The Great North Wales Loop

This is a 'Great Train Journey' type of outing rather than a ride on a tourist line or a mainline journey with a proper destination. Only very serious enthusiasts of rail travel would ever want to travel the whole loop in one go. However, for anyone who likes rail travel, but not enough to just sit on one train after another, the loop can offer a very interesting and enjoyable 'rail break'. Being a loop you can begin your journey by joining the train wherever you like. And when you look at some of the places you will pass through the idea of a holiday by rail, taking breaks as you want them, may seem a very attractive 'do-it yourself' option. I will describe the journey as it would be beginning and ending in Shrewsbury because that gets us straight into Wales and leaves the completely English section from Chester back to Shrewsbury until last which is just as it should be in a book entitled *Welsh Railways*!

Leaving Shrewsbury the train runs along the Cambrian Line which follows the Severn valley. There is now a well-marked long-distance footpath alongside the Severn established by the Environmental Agency, in conjunction with the County Councils of those shires through which the river passes. The train can be a useful way of getting on and off the path and enjoying the walk along this part of the river. The first stop is Welshpool, the home of the Welshpool and Llanfair Light Railway. It is a busy centre for this agricultural area and used to be a famous bottleneck for road traffic before a bypass was built. The rather lovely former station is now a restaurant.

The train runs on, never far from the Severn, through quiet, pleasant farmland much inhabited by rabbits and eventually arrives at Newtown. Newtown is a fairly big town but has no great charm and is functional rather than attractive. Much the same could be said about the next stop, Caersws, except that it is not very big at all. For the keen walker the distance from Caersws up to Plynlimon and back is only about six miles, just a short stroll really. The train leaves the Severn behind and heads off through the Cambrian mountains, sharing the route with the A470 trunk road, towards Machynlleth. It joins the Dovey valley and follows the river into the town.

Machynlleth is a pleasant little town but, unfortunately, the station is rather open and wind swept and not very near to the centre of the town. This is a pity because you will have to change trains here and there will probably not be time to walk into town. If the wait is at all long it will be a bit bleak unless the sun shines and the day is warm. The next stop is Dovey Junction, where the train you have left will have turned south and travelled down the other side of the estuary and on to Aberystwyth. You will head north, crossing the river, and run on beside the estuary towards the pretty resort town of Aberdovey. The Dovey estuary and all the countryside about is very attractive and surprisingly well-served by the weather as the variety and abundance of vegetation shows.

Aberdovey has long sandy beaches, views across the estuary, plenty of places to eat and stay and a fine links golf course. The train runs on, hugging the shore line, through a host of small coastal stations with views inland of Cader Idris. At Fairbourne the train runs across the long bridge in the beautiful Mawddach estuary. From the bridge you can see the station and café on Penrhyn Point belonging to the Fairbourne Light Railway. Across the Mawddach is Barmouth, a popular resort.

Beyond Barmouth the train again stays by the coast with views across the sea to the Lleyn Peninsula on clear days and views inland of the Snowdon mountains. The best-known place you will pass through is Harlech where the great castle still stands attracting visitors throughout the year. The train now begins to pull away from the coast to cross the river just before Penrhyndeudraeth. The bridge is shared with a road but drivers must pay a toll to use it. The train will now go on to Porthmadog and then along the south coast of the Lleyn Peninsula before finally arriving at its terminus at Pwllheli.

Not far from Porthmadog is Portmeirion, a sort of fantasy village built in an elaborate style and a very popular tourist attraction. You will leave the train at Porthmadog which is a bustling seaside town well-worth a visit. Porthmadog is also the coastal terminus of the train which will take you on the next part of your journey along one of Wales' restored and preserved lines, the Ffestiniog Railway.

The Ffestiniog Railway

The Ffestiniog Railway is rather wonderful. It is not just that it runs up from the coast into some of the most spectacular mountain scenery in Wales, which, of course it does. Rather it is because it does not fit in very well with the 'preserved railway' idea, although it is indeed a preserved railway, one of the earliest in fact. What makes the Ffestiniog Railway different is that the people who run it and the railway itself are actually going somewhere.

You can be a jolly tripper and go up and down the railway, from Porthmadog to Blaenau Ffestiniog, treating it as a great day out on a steam-hauled, narrow-gauge ex-quarry line. If you do, you will certainly get your money's worth in views alone. But, when you are on this tourist line, you are also on a part of the national rail system. This little preserved line is part of the rail link which joins the North Wales coast line to the main West Wales coast line. Llandudno Junction is on the main line from Chester to Holyhead, and Porthmadog is on the Cambrian line which serves the whole of the West Wales coast.

Backs of houses...

Without the Ffestiniog Railway there wouldn't be a Great North Wales Loop! The line is not just preserved, it is working and growing. The Ffestiniog Railway was behind the re-opening of the Welsh Highland Railway. That ambitious project is aimed at re-opening the old line from Caernarfon to Porthmadog both as a tourist line and a local service line. The people at the Ffestiniog Railway seem to believe that there is a future in re-opening railway lines; more, they seem enthusiastic about railway travel as a good way of getting about!

The Ffestiniog Railway, through their Porthmadog office, run one of the best railway booking-services available. And it isn't just railway travel in Britain they provide; you can book Eurostar tickets, European tickets, they even offer a worldwide railway-holidays service. The effort, enthusiasm and success of the Ffestiniog Railway take them quite out of the 'little railways of Wales' image into a 'railway – the way to travel' world. And they seem to be succeeding rather well.

The original railway was established in the 1830s to bring slate down from the Blaenau Ffestiniog quarries to the harbour at Porthmadog. The harbour itself and the town which grew up around it dates from 1821 when Parliament gave permission for a harbour to be built. The embankment along which the quarry line runs to its harbour terminus was built in the early part of the 19th century by William Alexander Maddocks M.P., thereby reclaiming between 7 and 10,000 acres of land around the Glaslyn estuary.

Tremadoc, far older than Porthmadog, lies on the western part of the estuary. It is said to have been founded by Madog ap Owen Gwynedd whose preferred form of transport was boat. Tradition has it that he set sail from nearby Ynys Fadog for America long before Columbus. Camel was the preferred form of transport of another famous local, T. E. Lawrence, Lawrence of Arabia, who was born in Tremadoc at a house called Woodlands. This area does seem to inspire a great enthusiasm for travel. The beauty of the area is also inspiring and it comes as no surprise to find that Shelley lived about ¾ of a mile from what became Porthmadog during 1812-13.

The railway runs from the coast up the Vale of Ffestiniog, climbing into

...,mountain ranges.

the Snowdon range. Tan y Bwlch, a station on the journey, has for long been a starting point for anyone who wishes to climb one of the local peaks, Moelwyn, which is 2527ft high. Blaenau Ffestiniog should not be confused with the actual village of Ffestiniog three miles away.

Anywhere given over to slate quarrying cannot usually claim any intrinsic beauty, even once the quarries have fallen silent. But the country all around is very beautiful indeed. Lord Lytton wrote of it, "with the woman one loves, with the friend of one's heart and a study of books one might pass an age in the vale and think it a day".

Even without the man or woman one loves, friends or a rucksack full of books, the Ffestiniog Railway is a wonderful place to visit for a day or to travel on towards the North Wales coast or, for the real rail enthusiast, to think of buying tickets to places far more foreign and exotic than Llandudno Junction.

From Blaenau Ffestiniog you are back on the main line. This part of the journey continues the trip over the mountains of the Snowdon range. Coming out of the long tunnel which begins the journey you pass through almost empty high land and among the spectacular scenery of the Snowdon National Park. After the mountains' stations the line joins the steep valley which holds the upper reaches of the River Conwy and the train runs on to the well-known visitor centre Betws-y-coed. Betws-y-coed is a centre for walkers and climbers and is home to the famous Swallow Falls and it is busy all the year round. The train runs on alongside the beautiful river and the valley becomes more gentle until the estuary is reached and the train pulls into Llandudno Junction.

On the far side of the estuary stands the mighty Conway castle with its many towers. The main line runs just under the castle walls carrying the trains from Holyhead in Anglesey and at Conway they pass over the river on Thomas Telford's wonderful suspension bridge which blends in so well with the castle that you could almost believe that the railway was Norman as well as the castle!

Now the main line will run along the North Wales coast through places whose names were once synonymous with summer holidays for countless thousands from the industrial West Midlands and Lancashire. They came in the 1950s and 60s before cheap air fares took them all off to the Costas and beyond. Colwyn Bay, Rhyl, Prestatyn: this whole coast was once lined with holiday camps and there are still acres of caravans to be seen from the train.

It is easy to see why so many came and still come to this part of Wales. It has great charm and beauty and just inland are sights such as the great fortress of Rhuddlan brooding darkly over the river Clwyd. Now a tourist attraction it is a reminder that the traffic in these parts for many centuries of its history was not that of holiday-making but of war. The castles and the many fine churches tell of a time when terrible violence and deep piety could sit side by side and death, heaven and hell were all very close to life.

The train runs on along the coast and past the wide Dee estuary. Across the estuary is the finger of England known as the Wirral with the Mersey estuary beyond. Once past Flint castle the train approaches the great fortified border city of Chester. The city of Chester is well-worth a visit although it long ago outgrew the defensive walls which now enclose only the centre of the city.

From Chester the next and final stage of your journey will cross and recross the Welsh/English border and, for the most part, be through gentle farmland and hills. The first stop will be Wrexham, a regional centre and busy industrial town. After Wrexham the train runs on to Ruabon and soon after crosses the

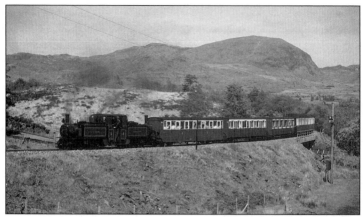

Through the sunshine to a happy ending.

Dee valley on a high viaduct. At the far end of this deep valley there is another great viaduct. It is the aquaduct that carries the Llangollen Canal which will wind its way out of Wales and cross Shropshire to join the Shropshire Union Canal just above Nantwich in Cheshire. The train runs along not far from the canal on its way to Chirk where it crosses another deep valley, that of the river Ceiriog. Both the train and the canal go through tunnels after Chirk station to come out into the Ceiriog valley which they cross in tandem, over the river far below, by two viaducts standing side by side and giving wonderful views. Now the canal wanders away eastwards and the train runs on to Gobowen. Gobowen is a small place but the station can be quite busy. It is the nearest station to Oswestry, an important local centre across the border in England.

After Gobowen the line itself is soon in England as it crosses into Shropshire, the largest of the English inland shires. The country is quietly beautiful and sparsely populated. Shropshire, such a beautiful and varied county, is comparatively little-known compared to its Marcher neighbours like Cheshire, Herefordshire and Worcestershire. Now the train rapidly approaches the county town of the shire, Shrewsbury, where the Great North Wales Loop was begun and will end. For anyone who can make this long journey it will be a wonderful experience of Welsh Railways.

**– Wales within your reach:
an attractive series
at attractive prices!**

1. Welsh Talk
Heini Gruffudd
086243 447 5
£2.95

2. Welsh Dishes
Rhian Williams
086243 492 0
£2.95

3. Welsh Songs
Lefi Gruffudd (ed.)
086243 525 0
£3.95

4. Welsh Mountain Walks
Dafydd Andrews
086243 547 1
£3.95

5. Welsh Organic Recipes
Dave and Barbara Frost
086243 574 9
£3.95

6. Welsh Railways
Jim Green
086243 551 X
£3.95

7. Welsh Place Names
Brian Davies
086243 514 5
£3.95

8. Welsh Castles
Geraint Roberts
086243 550 1
£3.95

9. Welsh Rugby Heroes
Androw Bennett
086243 552 8
£3.95

Also to be published in the *It's Wales* series:

Welsh National Heroes

Welsh History

Welsh Jokes

Learn the basics of the Welsh language:
**Written by the experienced author and
language tutor, Heini Gruffudd**

£2.95
ISBN: 0 86243 477 5

Also by Heini Gruffudd:
A fully illustrated introduction to the history, language, politics and
culture of Wales

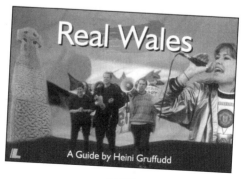

£4.95
ISBN: 0 86243 422 3

Welsh History:

A masterful history of the Welsh nation by the most distinguished Welsh politician of the twentieth century; 500 pages.

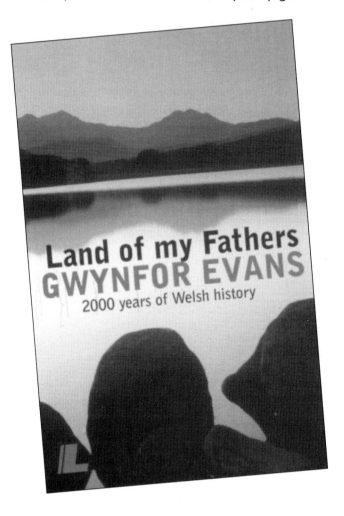

£12.95
ISBN: 0 86243 265 0

The *It's Wales* series
is just one of a wide range
Welsh interest publications
from Y Lolfa.
For a full list of books currently in print,
send now for your free copy
of our new, full-colour Catalogue
– or simply surf into our website
at **www.ylolfa.com.**

Talybont Ceredigion Cymru/*Wales* SY24 5AP
ffôn 0044 (0)1970 832 304 *ffacs* 832 782 *isdn* 832 813
e-bost ylolfa@ylolfa.com *y we* www.ylolfa.com